T0117142

The Blind Man Sees
What the Mute Man Tells

The Blind Man Sees
What the Mute Man Tells

Gabrielle Ayeni

authorHOUSE®

AuthorHouse™
1663 Liberty Drive
Bloomington, IN 47403
www.authorhouse.com
Phone: 1-800-839-8640

Published by AuthorHouse   11/26/2012

ISBN: 978-1-4685-3940-0 (sc)
ISBN: 978-1-4685-3939-4 (e)

Library of Congress Control Number: 2012900034

Contents

Life

Love

Society

Preface

Welcome to this journey of poetic expression. To give you a bit of background on myself, I have been writing poetry since I was a child and this book is a compilation of reflections, experiences, and people I have encountered throughout my life. Some poems are based on my impressions, some based on personal experience, and some are purely fictional based on passing strangers and imagining their stories. I hope you enjoy reading these poems as much as I have enjoyed writing them.

Dedication

This book is dedicated to my family, thank you for your continued support throughout the years. As I have grown and developed my writing you always encouraged me and I can never thank you enough for your support.

Life

Poetic Justice

I want to make similes shake
And metaphors mourn
I want to paint you with emotions you'd sworn
You'd never feel
And through puzzling pentameter
I want to shake up the parameters
Of all you once knew
My soul bleeds through the ink
Each letter a piece of me, I own it
And if only for a moment
I hope you escape to my world
Devoid of expectations
But full of imagination
Lacking organization
Yet full of clarity
Recognize the rarity
As I contradict diction
And defy proper rhyme
Yet my purpose will be divine
As long as you can still find
Your way to my world
So let your mind be your guide
And listen with your eyes
As you slip into lyrical paradise

Ashes In the Doldrums

Huddled masses
Over wooden caskets
You've been washed in the blood
And down their cheeks
Over sinewy peaks
Their tears rush like a flood
Through labored breaths
I watch your chest
Not rise and fall with mine
And as I glance back
It brings me back
As I see everyone fall in line
They glance in the casket
That terrible wooden basket
And all are take aback
And are quite aghast
Of what they've just seen
They somehow feel deceived
Their minds not wanting to believe

And in the back near the wall
A sobbing mother slowly falls
And softly lets out a wail
For she cannot believe this is her very own tale
That's real as real can be
And a terribly shocking reality
That you're not here with me
And as everyone's eyes begin to melt
Every soul deeply felt
A panging of despair
For this pain is one that we all must share
And with each morning dew
Signifying the day anew
I ask myself—why you?

Forecasting

My greatest fear has never been inadequacy
I've accepted my own rarity
Rather I fear the ever-encumbering complacency
But I got plenty of security
So my future will never be declined
And to protect me from an economy abating
So I don't just let life pass me by
I got a Triple-A bond rating
And if dreams were portfolios, best believe I diversified
No social safety net need I rely
Nor shall I be lulled into repose
When I make up my mind
It cannot be foreclosed
I will not allow Freddie Mac to back
Aspirations that are merely subprime
Look at the liquidity of my rhyme
Nothing short of sublime
Because I bought stock in the moon
And secured the rest in the stars
The forecast of my galaxy is above par

The Last Pas de Deux

I am a woman
I am a mother
I am a wife
I am a child of God
And I am beautiful

I must repeat these things in the mirror
As I begin to see things a little clearer
I must tell myself that I am whole
And I must convince myself that I believe
Despite it all I am complete
I must remind myself of this
As I hear the superficial remainder
Of my femininity—fall in front of my child's face
I must remind myself that my womanhood
Is still in place
And I am whole—even with this hole in my chest
I must remember as a joyful berry picking
Family outing
Quickly jolts me back to my reality
As I swiftly reach down
Without a sound, dust off my pride
And now berry-stained feminine prosthetic
Which glancing into the past year
Is nothing but prophetic

Of God's purpose to keep me here
I must remember as I fight back a tear
When it seems another piece of my world
Has fallen in an instant
That I just came within inches
Of this poison destroying my world
But I am still here

I am a woman
I am a mother
I am a wife
I am a child of God
And I am beautiful

See my mastectomy
Was the trajectory
To get me back on the right path
Refocused on what's important
No longer needing to keep up with the joneses
And now just needing to stop and smell the roses
I must remember where I am and where I was
I must find the good
I must still believe God is good
And would not give me more than I can bear
So though the right side of my chest is bare
I have weathered the storm

My life has been spared
And I have come back from deaths door
Through my exemption
I was blessed with redemption
And now I know for sure
That my friends, my family, my faith can endure
Whatever ill I run into
And I am stronger than I ever knew
And despite it all I have come through
Revitalized with a new point of view
Yes I've danced my last pas de deux
But I am here

I am a woman
I am a mother
I am a wife
I am a child of God
And I am STILL beautiful

Away

In your brief time here
You left great memories and a trail of tears
You taught us all about selfless love
A gift from above
Your never-ending love never needed to be returned
But in the end you still got burned

I cry tears of joy in your passing
For your love was everlasting
But maybe you escaped the disease's pain
Worn down from the strain
Of having the world's judgment on your shoulders
Day after day having to climb boulders
For some people love wasn't enough
Searching for gold they missed a diamond in the rough

The "American Dream" has turned man's heart to stone
Now forced to roam
This land in search of a gold mine
It's mansions not love they must find
Despite how kind
You were

One glad morning,
When this life is over,
I'll fly away

Like an angel from above
You spread your love
While persecution ran like a flood
Despite each new drop of blood
That signaled you would be leaving soon
The greedy thieves came like a monsoon
And not a tear they shed
But wanted every dime you had
Loving memories had no place in their minds
They just wanted every dime
They could get their hands on
No matter what the cost—you being gone
And with your last breath
They asked for the keys to your treasure chest
But when you needed a hand
To escape the angel of death they ran and ran
Until they heard you fall
And realized death sucked the honey of thy breath
Somehow it doesn't seem fair
But then maybe God planned for you
To escape your pain in eternal rest
He would never give you more than you could bear
So one glad morning you flew away
I know that you are finally okay
Because one glad morning you flew away
Away, away, away

Zombie Train

Steady as she goes
Steady as she goes
Steady as she rolls
Steady as you know
Steady as she goes

This train it rolls
The stops everyone knows
Doors closing
Are you going to be late again?
Slip through that turnstile with ease
Its muscle memory performing the morning routine
To the next stop it rolls
Passengers slip into a lull
No worries for the moment
It's a rare bit of peace
But it's crashing soon and you know it
Brace for impact
Screech of the rails
It's your stop
And you know it far too well
The moment is gone
But this train will go on

Steady as she goes
Steady as she goes

The wind rushes in
With next batch of passengers

What's your story I wonder?
The man with the paper
Or the kid with headphones
Each one a character
Carrying a story their own
Many passengers the same
But not one knowing another's name
It's too early for pleasantries
It's too cold to be nice
Too hot to make friends
No need to pretend
Just open your book or paper
And dig your head in
Close your eyes and slip into nirvana
Your body has an internal alarm
No need for any concerns
Drift into sleep as the zombie train rolls on

Steady as she goes
Steady as she goes
Steady as she rolls
Steady as you know
The Zombie train it rolls
Steady as she goes

What's the cure for poverty?
How can we save humanity from society?
Why is the quest for power so deadly?
Who the hell knows?
But I know one constant that stays the same
Like clockwork baby it's the zombie train

Lifecycles

The dew that drips
The soul that rips
The child who trips
Is it all the same?
How does it change?
What happens to the remains?

It seems that we often seek the perfect ending
But is it actually endings we seek?
Or does the true joy actually lie in the journey?
For the journey has
Better obstacles
Better connections
Sweeter intentions
Better ability to live in the moment
Greater sense of atonement
Better ability to trust
More love and less lust
Better lives
And less sad memories
All this can be attained in the journey

For I feel that it is not in our implications
But in our daily relations
And willingness to change
The path we are going on
That we find our true joy
And stop trying to run

Yin and Yang

Nothing is anything without the antithesis
And that dichotomy defines everything
We are happy only because we know
The depths of sadness
Thus man can never be content to exist
Solely in paradise
The pendulum of happiness
Swings on a tenuous string

Those who have lived too long in the shadows
Bask in the white-hot light
But that happiness is restrained
Because they know the nearness of the night

Now those who have never experienced the darkness
Do not know enough to appreciate the light
The sun burns, and begins to feel rather contrite
And any shadow cast feels like the darkest night

It is a beautiful catastrophe,
This thing we call life,
We know we exist because we have seen others die
With the pleasure of a touch
Comes the pain of giving life
And in the sadness of death we know we are alive

Caution: Contents Under Pressure

A picture of perfection
Yet it is all a deception
Pretty picture painted
Yet it's secretly been tainted

Tell me why I feel depressed
When life is supposed to be the best
But it is spinning out of control
I don't even know my role
It's my car that I always ride
Shouldn't I learn to drive?
Instead of being content to sit
Getting lit and flipped
Cruising without a hitch

I have to be perfect
I must work it
No place to fail
I must prevail
All emotions kept in jail
And reality veiled
Contents under pressure
I have to measure
Up to and exceed every expectation
No matter what path must be taken
Regardless I will be making it
In this world because failure is not an option
Aspirations of mediocrity must be forgotten

Point, Click, Type, Send

I'm in a circular prison,
Filled with cubicle walls and ergonomic keyboard living
That is something like a prism
Illuminating my worst fears
Because this unpaid internship
Feels one oar short of a slave ship
As I watch myself slip
Into a monotonous trend
Point . . . click . . . type . . . send
Sleep wake up and restart again

You have a status on that spreadsheet?
Cackle of the ball and chain
Jolts me back from an important net surfing daydream
Visualize shutting down for good
All the while letting my hands
Work the keyboard like the trained monkey I am
Have to get that out by close of business today!
Freeing up my afternoon for a brief moment of web surfing
tranquility
Before it all begins again
Point . . . click . . . type . . . send
Sleep wake up restart again

Ghosts Passing Through

In every face I see
Walking down the street
And every time I think
Or even pause to blink
You're with me
Even in my mind
I cannot seem to find
A place where I am free

Well you can't haunt my heart
You had me hiding in the dark
But I have to let go
Of the pain you made me feel
That was deeper than the wounds that healed
You came in the night and stole, ruptured my soul
And no one knows but me
Truthfully who would believe?

This emptiness is real
But my perseverance is stronger still
My soul cannot be invaded
My heart will not be dissuaded
So when I see your face in the streets
I no longer need to retreat
I keep walking by
I will never again hide from you
Because you are just a ghost passing through

Pause

Now I know in the grand scheme of things
This is merely a blip on the radar
I know it's not that bad
But right now I can't see the land
And right now I'm not in the state of mind
To have a never you mind state of mind
I just want a free minute
To wallow in my sorrows and indecision
I just want a carefree minute
Don't judge me by my present disposition
See everyone has a time
When you want to just stop in time
And pass on the "everything is fine" state of mind

No, I don't need a couch or a handful of pills
This pen is better than Ambien
And all who listen hold the only Ph.D.s I need
So just let me float with the current
Because any second I will be jolted back from my current
Place of sweet misery
Forced to put on a smile
To avoid pesky questions
From those with feigned good intentions
And with each smile I accept my denial
As I let my true emotions pile
And in this moment,
I have never more envied the pure happiness of a child

Beachcombing

I waited until I saw the sun
I don't know why you didn't come
Walked the earth to find the world at home
You were here all along

An empty shell
Is what you've become
The remnant shell
Of a bullet fired, a war won
Your heart's percussion remains
But your soul's conductor has left the train

When I see you now
I struggle to remember
The man you used to be
But I've come to a place where I can see
Past your present to your beautiful memory

Seeing you in such physical purgatory
Made me question God's obligatory plan
Because all I saw was a shell
Looked in to the eyes of an apparition of a man
Then dusted off all the sand
To reveal a conch in my hand
Reminding me that once a sea creature leaves this land
We are not left with the pain
Rather only the beautiful remains

So now when I walk the beach
And feel a smooth shell beneath my feet
I feel you in the breeze off the sea
Each wave bringing a new piece of you to me

Love

Star Gazing

A warm night with clear blue skies
Far beneath entranced we lie
And in that moment nothing else exists
Besides us and our cool brown lips

Mind Travels in the Sky

And there we were just lost in ourselves
Floating about aimlessly
Trying to figure out where we'd rather be

There are so many questions that I have unanswered
And now I wonder
Is there a place where I can be
Just myself and nobody else
Live truly free,
And this fog in my head is evident
That this moment was meant to be

Floating about the constellation
I look at him with consternation
Wondering if this could be a mutation
Because my feelings have transformed themselves
And now I love somebody else
But it's too hard tell him there's someone I'd rather see
See in my heart there's so much distraction
Working to figure out his reaction
And trying to remember my initial attraction
Suddenly I am only filled with apathy
How did we let our love atrophy?

As the bell ominously tolls
I'm filled with surprising serenity
Yes, I know what the future holds
But I'd rather float in the clouds and let it be

A New Day

I've cried these tears
And let them fall
My soul is clear
I'm through with it all
Now, I'm moving on

Each step I take
Each day anew
I start thinking less about you
Because after all it's over now
Love's thorny crown has fallen down
We've taken our last bow

I just thought you were the one somehow
It seems so silly now
After all you're right it seems,
We were just a couple of kids with big dreams
And now I can see
That we were never meant to be

Poison Tree

*Collaboration with Jared Culp

I need your love
You feed my soul
My poison tree
Come back to me

Your poison is my fuel
Even though you can be so cruel
For some reason I keep coming back for more
And I know
Oh I know that things will not go as I planned
But I don't even have to make you mine
I just want a little bit of your time
Because you're always on my mind
And I'll take any piece of you
That you're willing to give
So for those brief moments my heart can live

Life without you hasn't been great
No love and no hate
But an infinite number of meaningless relationships
That fall between the cracks
And they still don't bring you back

So here I am now
Open as can be
Pleading desperately to get you back
And sad as it may sound I don't even
Have to have your heart
Just being with you makes me feel better
Plus I know
That deep down inside
Behind that loser you're hooking up with
That you feel something between us
So I'll be here
Waiting to wipe your tears
Waiting for us to learn how to really communicate
Waiting for the scars to heal
Waiting for you to find your way back to my arms
And this time I will be ready
To protect you from all harm
And this time, I mean me too
Because I know I hurt you the most

I need your love
You feed my soul
My poison tree
Come back to me
And in the end
I'd do it again
You're my weakness
Baby you're my sin
And we weren't meant to be just friends

I Thought I Could Swim

I took off down the road
With no map in my hand
Gave up on searching for water
Felt safer on land

And there he was six foot fine
Sly smile and hazel holes for eyes
Told my legs to keep walking
But my heart wouldn't oblige
Told myself to be cool
Still I felt my temperature rise
Because you gave me a look
That made this chocolate beauty blush
Felt a shot of warmth through my cheeks
I've never felt so flushed

Tried to play it close to the vest
But I've never had much of a poker face
And I don't know how but you can call my bluff
Before I knew it I'd tripped right in
Those deep pools in your eyes
And I thought I could swim

Stand

When I see you fall
I want to call out and save you
But all I feel is your face
Slipping from my loving embrace

Try as I might
We will always fight
Because I can't be the one
To shine your sun
You have to find your light within
To escape your self-made prison

I want to save you
I want to make you whole again
I want to make you right again
I want to make you happy within
But all this has shown
That it's time for you to stand on your own

Cardiac Arrest

Tonight I'm yours
Tonight you're mine
There is no after or before
Let's enjoy this reckless game once more

We've blurred the line
Of reality and insanity
But the reason escapes me
Why I continue entertaining
And you continue engaging
Me into this dangerous game of pretend
But what happens when fake becomes real
Does real become fake?

I await the answer as the dawn breaks
Illuminating our mistakes
Who is to say believing is in seeing
When the light sheds understanding
And replaces passion with confusion
For now I will lie in your arms in reckless delusion
Each kiss a cardiac contusion

The Blind Man Sees
What the Mute Man Tells

You never had to tell a lie
You never had to say goodbye

Your eyes decried
All the vows you defied
And now you wear your guilt on your sleeve
Right where your heart used to be

In the silent nights
And tear free rains
I realize we will never be the same
Because I see the string of broken promises
On your neck like a tattoo in the form of a kiss
And the shape of those lips
Will burn a hole in my heart forever

It's time for each of us to have a fresh start
We've already fallen apart
Now we are just holding on to the past
But in the dark I see it will never last
Your touch, your eyes, they say it all
As I hear the clang of the ring fall
You never had to tell a lie
You never had to say goodbye

Seasons

I fall in love like the seasons
And I would really like to settle down
If the right weather pattern could give me a reason
But until then I will happily
Spring into love with my heart on my sleeve
Of this season's cardigan
And watch it melt away and fizzle
As a new summer love makes my heart sizzle
Until it falls like the leaves
As my heart begins to flutter for another
Before being frozen in time
As I coolly melt into a new lover's embrace and he becomes mine
And I am so calm as the new one gets waived on
But still each one leaves an abrasion
A remnant of the past and a lesson for the future
So the next heart rupture will take less sutures
Yet the pain is anesthetized by the beauty of the seasons
Each solstice my heart breathes a sigh of freedom

Icarus's Love

For you I would paint our names on the sun
And burn a lasting image of our love
In the hearts and souls of every man
So when they sleep and darkness creeps
They won't unravel at the seams
For our love will keep them company in their dreams

Society

Popular Musings

Degradation was reduced to entertainment
At the hands of this pop culture nation
Nigga this nigga that
A past forgotten at the drop of a hat
Dollar signs erasing
A past humiliation
And condescension rising
Faster than feigned social status climbing
See we split hairs over Imus
But I must admit
We don't talk much better amongst ourselves
How can we expect love from another
When we cannot show it to our own brothers?
And I realize that these are the unlikely
Futile cries of another
Hold your head high though
For the pride of a broken mother

Overexposed

Overexposure was the cause of death,
But the elements didn't get her yet,
It was the celebrity cribs and the OC,
Got so caught up couldn't tell what was
Reality from TV,
And started to believe everything I'd see

Overexposure was the cause of death,
The flashbulb even ripped through my chest,
The negative was all that was left,
And the only thing to speak truth in the mess,
Somehow the streaks were the perfect effect

Smile for the camera,
Hide in the light,
There's no need to fight tonight

Overexposure was the cause of death
The ads and lies resonated
It got in my mind couldn't escape it
Poisoned my dreams and everywhere I turn
I'd open up my eyes but I cannot stand the burn

Overexposure was the cause of death
And I wonder if we are passing the test
When the abundance of ads targeted at teens
Results in drastically increased consumption
And living beyond means
Exposing that this isn't an arms race it's a damn scene

Smile for the camera,
Hide in the light,
There's no need to fight tonight
The flashes make everything alright

Overexposure was the cause of death,
And through it all nothing disturbed your rest,
Not quite in peace, but you managed to keep,
Up the appearance and with the calmness of a priest,
I finally understood your blank stare,
Your voice spoke through your eyes,
"Let go and let God, Laissez-faire"

Martyr of Society

I can't stand the pain
Of another drop of rain
Another piece of mold
Attacking my soul

I can't stand the pain
Of another drop of rain
I'll never gain fame
My life is full of shame

And I can't stand the pain
Of another drop of rain
I can't even stand
My life is a sham

And I can't stand the pain
Of another drop of rain
This one piece of lead
Will soon control my head

As I sit on this bed
The only thoughts in my head
Are about this one piece of lead

With my pen in my hand and a gun in the other
I start to think about my sorry mother
And all the pain she put me through
Well mama its time for you to pay your dues

As I stare at the blank sheet of paper,
I start thinking about how we used to sneak in the store and
watch the Lakers
As I look down at the pen in my hand I start to think about
how this all began
I was born on the streets, quite an insignificant birth,
But still don't I belong on this earth?

Oh how society is fickle
They'll mourn me tomorrow
But what about today?
I won't even get a nickel

Forget that I won't even get a decent funeral
What hurts me the most is that no one can see who I am
O Lord why must I be damned?

See what you seem to forget
Is that I have no regrets
You walk by full of anger and pity
How could you even purse your lips to spit on me?
Don't condemn me for my parent's mistakes
This isn't the path I chose to take

Bye, bye now, it's time for me to go
And maybe my death will finally show
That we are human beings
No matter how spurned our birth
It still doesn't give you a reason to treat us like dirt
Mama you did this with your pipes and your pimps
Forcing me to start my life with a limp

Daddy thanks a lot
For leaving us here to rot

And I can't stand the pain
Of another drop of rain
Because I got the weight of the world on my shoulders
And I'm still climbing over boulders
The scarlet drops of my blood
Rush from my head like an endless flood
All I wanted was a little love
Why couldn't somebody give it up?
And I hope that you soon will see
That I didn't die for nothing
Yea, I didn't die for nothing

Lost Souls of the Ghetto

How can we catch the ones who fall?
Is there a way to save them all?

It's ingrained in the persevering nature of every
African-American
The culture runs deep and through
This needle going into
Your arm
And even though you know it will harm you
Its power is stronger than the pain
Of the this needle going into your vein
And you daughter's cries are in vain
Because you never came
And it's too hard to explain
Why daddy's not here to help
You both get through the rain
Instead of back here again
It is far too hard to fight the devil within
That has taken on the form of an addiction
But it's okay the drip, drip, drip of the gin
Will wash away all these sins

See you watched another day go by
Busy trying to get high
Or find a good fix
While your poor baby hid in the corner
Just watching the clock go tick, tock, tick
Wondering how long her mommy is gonna

Let her tongue go click, click, click
And scratch until there is nothing left to pick
And you are so numb you can't even feel
The needle's prick

See the dealer can't cure you,
But he will lure you
Away from all your good intentions
And ruin all the purity
Of your daughter who is now a mother-to-be
Not even thirteen
She can't see her own inner strength and beauty
Too blind from her mother's pain
And all these years of rain
She feels that the storybook cannot change
Or even focus with a gin soaked brain
And yields to the needle's pain
As the ghetto lays claim
Of another lost soul continuing the chain

How can we catch the ones who fall?
Is there a way to save them all?

Reparations Ain't For Me

Reparations ain't for me
Now don't think I've made this decision blindly
I just have my own dream

See reparations ain't for me
Because I do not understand how money
Can be equated to appease the effects and pain of slavery
What is the price of a man's life?
Because I cannot put a price on their pain,
their struggle, their strife
Their blood and tears fell down like rain
They fertilized the soil with their pain
They were the ones who were brutalized with canes
This wasn't my struggle but it is my pain
And I cannot see using it merely for pecuniary gain
See their pain doesn't have a fee
They died to help us be free
All the while shaping me into me
Affording us the chance to be all we can be
So you see reparations ain't for me
Because I am not deserving

Since when have you been so concerned
About getting paid?
Because last night your primary concern
Was getting laid
Indifferent to the fact that our new master
Is now self-made

And we have once again become slaves
Of this disease we call AIDS
Africa is still riddled with wars
And we're here sipping our Coors
If money is to be given to anything
Then why not help the dying,
Afflicted with pain and crying
Especially the little children
Who don't know why everyone is sighing
And we perpetuate the ignorance by lying
To ourselves about why we're literally
Or figuratively poor
But blaming it on the "white man"
Isn't going to cut it any more

Stand up and scream
Stop trying to lean
Dare to dream
Enjoy being free
Just do something to let me see
That like a light we'll put up a fight
And not go easily into the night
Show everyone we are still alive
Ready to dive
Into the pool of life and create our own dreams
Even break some seams
So hopefully now you can see
Just why reparations ain't for me
Because it won't recreate us into new beings
No amount of money is even redeeming
And frankly I'm disgusted at the thought

That after everything our ancestors went through,
And how hard they fought
Now their struggles can be bought
Which to me is nothing but a cheap after thought
That should have never been brought—
Up in the first place

Because we're all going to make a mark on the human race
God just set us on a different pace
So you see—reparations aint for me
Because no amount of money will ever be
Able to replace those who died valiantly
And left great memories
Yes reparations ain't for me
Because I have my own dream

So I urge you to stand up and scream
And join me,
In the fight for a better we
We might stumble,
Or almost crumble
But united as a culture
And more importantly, as human beings
We will stand tall
And I assure you we will not fall
As long as together we stand tall
We will not
And cannot fall

A Dream Affirmed

Lift every voice and sing
Till earth and heaven ring,
Ring with the harmonies of Liberty
Let our rejoicing rise
High as the listening skies,
Let it resound loud as the rolling sea.

I went to sleep and awoke to the American Dream
November 4, 2008 a day that will go down in history
And forever resonate in my soul
All the world rejoiced—as he gave voice
To the struggling cries of a nation
Dancing in the streets to mark the momentous occasion
A . . . new . . . world . . . order

Stony the road we trod,
Bitter the chastening rod,
Felt in the days when hope unborn had died;
Yet with a steady beat,
Have not our weary feet
Come to the place for which our fathers sighed?

Through the perilous fight that tested all our might
Each battle leading to this great night
An unimaginable journey that still continues
And a history wrought with shattered barriers
No Ellis Island memorial for these unknown heroes
Dragged here on ships

Backs bloodied but unbowed and unbroken
Despite the weight of the whips
Ashes to ashes and dust to dust
A past long gone but never forgotten at dusk
We toiled the acres and fought for every inch
There were those who harbored slaves forced to flee like
Refugees in our own country
Not even considered contributing members of society
And in those times strong leaders took stands
When this land was your land
This land was my land
And never ever OUR land
Stony the road we trod, yet our weary feet
Feel reborn celebrating on this night dancing
In the streets
For we have come on the backs of all those
Who passed before us
When the stars were the only free things in sight
That united us with the black cloth
That covered us each night
For we all could see the same white gleam
That burned bright
When the broad stripes and bright stars
Bled red, white, and blue but never brown

God of our weary years,
God of our silent tears,
Thou who has brought us thus far on the way;
Thou who has by Thy might
Led us into the light,
Keep us forever in the path, we pray.

From the steps of Little Rock
To the foothills of Birmingham
Yes we did

From three fifths of a person
To disenfranchised from a vote
Yes we did

On the backs of the weary
To the voice of a dream
Yes we did

From the Reconstruction era post of Joseph Rainey
To the pen of Fredrick Douglas
Yes we did

From the black codes of 1865
To the Jim Crow South
Yes we did

From Bacons Rebellion
To the fortitude of Quock Walker
Yes we did

From the courage of abolitionists
To each track Harriet Tubman laid
Yes we did

From Nat Turner's Rebellion
To Bleeding Kansas
Yes we did

From the disregarded rights of Dred Scott
To the sweat of Buffalo Soldiers
Yes we did

From the leadership of Booker T.
To the march of a million men
Yes we did

From the flout of Malcolm
To the peaceful vision of Martin
Yes we did

From the denied justice to Emmett Till
To the selection of Governor Pinchback
Yes we did

From the works of Shirley Chisholm
To the appointment of Colin Powell
Yes we did

Out of the trenches of slavery
And in the face of a devastated nation
The first black president elect
Of the United States of America
Barack Hussein Obama
An unlikely hero who gave voice to the forlorn
And hope to the weary
United across cultures
He gave birth to a new regime
With the simple creed
Yes we can

Yes we have been woven into the fabric of this country
From the first slave ship in 1619 to the first leader in 2008
We have heard "all men are created equal"
But today we felt the country's fundamental creed
Today we felt we belonged and finally believed
On November 4th I went to sleep
And awoke to the American Dream

Let us march on til victory is won
Til victory is won

Today I realize that only one national anthem
Need be sung
Today I retire the Negro national anthem
That led many heroes through perilous nights
Today, like Obama has demonstrated, we begin to turn the
other cheek
Today we are one people,
One nation,
Under God,
Indivisible,
With liberty,
And justice,
For all
Liberty and Justice for all

Today we have a new anthem
That speaks to the bright future of this nation
And not to the depths of the past
That rings from coast to coast and sea to sea

Yes we can
Repair this world
Yes we can

For in the unlikely story of America there has never been
anything false about hope

So Langston you queried what comes of a dream deferred
It doesn't dry up like a raisin in the sun
It swells to the unimaginable
The dream affirmed

I went to sleep and awoke to the American Dream
I went to sleep and awoke to the American Dream

The Contradiction of Addiction's Affliction

I'm addicted to this life
I'm trying to get by
Addicted to this life
Lying to survive
On these streets
Trying to make a living
I'm dying to make my way home

Now folks there's no need to be rude
It's been 3 days since this man's had solid food
Last 5 meals been straight booze
And now you're saying I have to choose
Between my daughter and the bottle
I don't know which is worse
The fact that I'm having trouble making a decision
Or that I have to choose at all because of this addiction

And I keep hearing about a war on poverty
But for some reason the troops haven't made their way to me
I know they are storming every soup kitchen and street
But for some reason the war plan is too discreet
And though we've tried with all our might
I think the government has won this fight
And everyday for me is a fight
Each day filled with so much strife
And every morning I ask God why he continued my life

See this daily struggle is so hard
Especially when I know meals
Are easier to come by behind bars
Seems funny
That in our society
You put two holes in a man's chest
And you get guaranteed meals
And sheltered place to rest
But me, I put one hole in my arm and one in my liver
And I am forced to shiver
Out in the cold because I don't fit the mold
Huddled under blankets with others like me
At the floor of society

Welcome to the South

Lay down your burden
Lay down your burden
Lay your head on my shoulder
And let the tears keep rolling
Baby lay down your burden

Age 8
Thrown into a place
Where apparently my race
Is considered inferior
And everything white superior
So confused was I
That I wasn't supposed to hang out
With Jesse or Sara
But play with Kareem
The other black child in our class
Which was so strange to me
Coming from Philly
Where we all played together
Hopscotch on the street
Dancing to the beat
And tap tap tapping our feet
But this was a new beat
It was time for this child to be
Introduced quite shockingly
To the South
And all stops to come out
Because I'm not white
Which apparently makes me not quite right

Now see sir
You seem to just be introducing me to the class
But it seems to me
That it's much more than that
You see this was my first meeting
With the South
Where all stops were pulled out
Much like you pulled me out
Of class
To tell me that I was no longer invited
To the honor society
And before I had a chance to see
Or find out why I was thrust back into class
After being embarrassed
And fighting back tears
That welled up for years
And told to keep
Pluck plucking my violin
Which wasn't even the instrument
I wanted to play
But all you would say
To me was that my lips
Were just too big for the flute
But I saw you sign off on all the white kids slips
All the while sending me to the to the string instruments
A place where my disfigured African anatomy
Would not be a problem
And I will pass this on to my son
And my son's son or daughter
And here I was thinking of them as beautiful
But that's alright I'll still push to be the best

And leave you with nothing but ignorance
And sins to confess

See because making it in that white school
Was like sitting on the front stool
At a whites only bar
Not even flinching when they threw tar
Ignoring their words but feeling their scars
But everyone has the right to aim for the stars
White kids are not the only ones who can go far
So sir you introduced the South to me
But you stand corrected, the South needed to meet me
And understand that this is how it is going to be

Leave no stone unturned
Let it all burn away
And just lay down
Baby lay down your burden

Another Candle Lit

Another candle lit
Another soul ripped
From life itself

Another candle lit
Another dream slips
Into the night

Another candle lit
Another day in a senseless fight

Another candle lit
Another child takes his first step

Another candle lit
Another father never sees his daughter's eyes

Another candle lit
Another mother never gets to say goodbye

Another candle lit
Another wave of propaganda fills our heads with lies

Another candle lit
And still no one will stand up and apologize

Eye for an eye
Eyes for the whole world blind
We must remove the log from our own eyes
Or watch this world crumble into demise